DUBLIN
THE CITY AT A GLANCE

Central Bank of Irelan
Irish architect Sam Step
finished in 1978, was hate
has only recently started t
See p070

City Hall
Thomas Cooley's 1770s excha
has been a meeting place for ..., s
aldermen since the 1850s, its giant portico
and copper dome dominating Temple Bar.
Dame Street, T 222 2204

O'Connell Bridge
A remnant of the high-Georgian improvements
made to Dublin, James Gandon's landmark
is the main crossing between the rundown
north and chichi south.

Ha'penny Bridge
The footbridge from a thousand postcards
takes you from a redeveloped quayside on
the north bank of the River Liffey into the
heart of the raucous Temple Bar.

Four Courts
Home to Ireland's Supreme Court, this is
Gandon's great domed gift to posterity,
bringing hints of Wren and Rome to Dublin.
See p010

General Post Office
The grandly porticoed site of the doomed
1916 Easter Rising, the GPO is decorated
with bullet holes.
See p015

The Spire
This is urban regeneration through the eye of
a 120m-high needle. Ian Ritchie's breathtaking
design pierces the skyline of this low-rise city.
See p013

INTRODUCTION
THE CHANGING FACE OF THE URBAN SCENE

There are a lot more tanned bodies and Range Rovers in Dublin than there used to be. This seems to be what happens when a poor, pale, freckly city experiences a decade and a half of phenomenal growth: everyone splashes out on luxury cars and trips to the beauty salon. Modern Dubliners clearly don't do stealth wealth. For the visitor, the economic miracle has delivered a host of classy hotels, high-style restaurants complete with world-class chefs and Michelin stars, and well-run, well-funded galleries and museums that justify a design-led trawl of the city. In fact, now is a great time to travel to Dublin: the air positively hums with energy and the locals have had plenty of time to adjust to their affluence.

Not everything has changed, though. The city's impressive range of architecture, from the wide streets and grand, romantic edifices of Georgian Dublin to the concrete of the postwar years and current regeneration of the Docklands area, remains highly viewable by foot, while the Irish capital's place in the history of modernism is starting to be appreciated. Meanwhile, the service industries may have been augmented by thousands of Baltic immigrants, but the new workforce has caught on quick to the city's reputation for friendliness and the human touch – the cliché of a thousand welcomes remains well pitched. And of course there is the wit, the Guinness and Dublin's legendary pubs. For many, these would be worth the trip alone.

ESSENTIAL INFO

FACTS, FIGURES AND USEFUL ADDRESSES

TOURIST OFFICE
Dublin Tourism Centre
Suffolk Street
T 605 7700
visitdublin.ie

TRANSPORT
Car hire
Avis
35-39 Old Kilmainham
T 605 7500
Murrays Europcar
2 Haddington Road
Baggot Street Bridge
T 614 2888
Trams
Luas
T 800 300 604
www.luas.ie
Taxis
Access Metro Cabs
T 668 3333
Castle Cabs
T 802 2222

EMERGENCY SERVICES
Ambulance/Fire/Police
T 999
Late-night pharmacy
Hamilton Long & Co
4 Merrion Road
T 668 3287

EMBASSIES
British Embassy
29 Merrion Road
T 205 3700
www.britishembassy.ie
US Embassy
42 Elgin Road
T 668 8777
dublin.usembassy.gov

MONEY
American Express
41 Nassau Street
T 890 205 511
www.americanexpress.ie

POSTAL SERVICES
Post Office
O'Connell Street
T 705 7000
Shipping
DHL
44 Sandwith Street Upper
T 890 725 725
dhl.ie

BOOKS
Dubliners by James Joyce (Penguin Modern Classics)
The Green Flag: A History of Irish Nationalism by Robert Kee (Penguin)
Scott Tallon Walker Architects: 100 Buildings and Projects, 1960-2005 by John O'Regan (Gandon Editions)

WEBSITES
Architecture
irish-architecture.com
Magazine
thedubliner.ie

COST OF LIVING
Taxi from Dublin Airport to city centre
£20
Cappuccino
£2
Packet of cigarettes
£6
Daily newspaper
£1.35
Bottle of champagne
£35

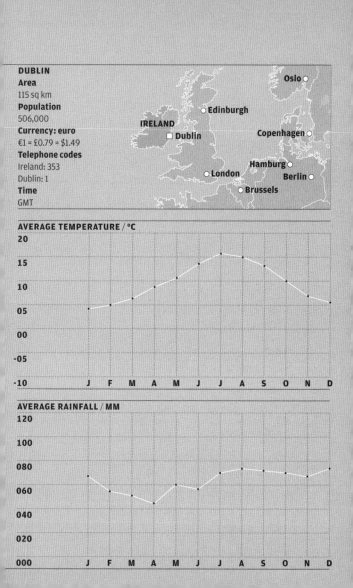

DUBLIN
Area
115 sq km
Population
506,000
Currency: euro
€1 = £0.79 = $1.49
Telephone codes
Ireland: 353
Dublin: 1
Time
GMT

Oslo
Edinburgh
IRELAND
Dublin
Copenhagen
Hamburg
London
Berlin
Brussels

AVERAGE TEMPERATURE / °C

20

15

10

05

00

-05

-10

J F M A M J J A S O N D

AVERAGE RAINFALL / MM

120

100

080

060

040

020

000

J F M A M J J A S O N D

NEIGHBOURHOODS
THE AREAS YOU NEED TO KNOW AND WHY

To help you navigate the city, we've chosen the most interesting districts (see below and the map inside the back cover) and colour-coded our featured venues, according to their location; those venues that are outside these areas are not coloured.

THE LIBERTIES AND KILMAINHAM

A pre-regeneration aesthetic prevails here, all fly-blown antiques shops, galleries and students idling in old men's boozers. The main draws are the Irish Museum of Modern Art (Military Road, T 612 9900) and the Guinness Storehouse (St James's Gate, T 408 4800), for a pint with a view.

CENTRAL SOUTH

Dublin's beating heart is where the city comes to shop, eat and party. Away from Grafton Street – the dull, chain-store centre – are quaint pubs, kooky boutiques, boho brasseries, members' clubs and gastro destinations such as Fallon & Byrne (see p048), where the beautiful hang out.

CENTRAL NORTH

Much has been spent on a plan to revive O'Connell Street with, among other things, the marvellously meaningless Spire (see p013), but north of the river remains a place to visit rather than base yourself. That said, the GPO (see p015) and Busáras (see p068) are not-to-be-missed landmarks.

GEORGIAN DUBLIN

The swanky squares and brick terraces don't just house lawyers, politicians and museums. Around St Stephen's Green and Baggot Street it's more epicurean, with Michelin-starred cuisine – L'Ecrivain (see p044) and Restaurant Patrick Guilbaud (see p051) – and the glammed-up cocktail crowd at The Shelbourne (see p026).

TRINITY COLLEGE

Through the Corinthian portico of the Trinity West Front entrance lie beetling students, quiet squares and some of the most dazzling architecture in the city, from the late 18th-century William Chambers-designed neoclassical Examination Hall to the sleek 2002 James Ussher Library (see p074).

DOCKLANDS

The anonymous, glass-fronted apartment blocks here will soon be joined by a central square designed by American landscape architect Martha Schwartz, a theatre by Daniel Libeskind and a 'chessboard' hotel by Manuel Aires Mateus located by the regenerated Grand Canal Dock.

RANELAGH AND BALLSBRIDGE

Dublin's southern suburbs have seen an eye-popping rise in house prices and an explosion of glitzy venues to serve the property Euromillionaires. Nothing screams new money meets old more than the chichi bar, skilled mixologists and ice-cool barflies at The Dylan (see p024).

TEMPLE BAR

What was once destined to be a giant bus station is Dublin's most famous party zone. It's not all hens and stags a-staggering along the cobbled lanes, though; look for classier corners, such as the restaurants and museums in Meeting House Square (see p066), or the high-end boutiques around Cow's Lane and Scarlett Row (see p082).

LANDMARKS

THE SHAPE OF THE CITY SKYLINE

Dublin has a wealth of imposing landmarks, not least of which is the relatively recent Spire (see p013). Controversial to some, because of its lack of meaning, and cheekily nicknamed the 'Stiffy by the Liffey' by locals, it has grown to be accepted as a symbol of Dublin's economic resurgence and marks an effort to bring some regeneration to the part of the city north of the river. But for most visitors, their excursions north won't take them much further than the Irish nationalist shrine of the GPO (see p015) or the Palladian splendour of the Four Courts (overleaf) and Custom House (see p014), both located on the water's edge.

Much of your stay is likely to be spent supping, shopping and strolling in the pleasant streets south of the Liffey. Slap-bang in the middle is Trinity College, whose West Front entrance onto College Green is one of the city's great meeting places, while its walled grounds teem with historic and modernist architectural inspiration (see p072 and p074). To the south, all is low-rise Georgian, miles of symmetry upset only by the odd Scott Tallon Walker or Sam Stephenson construction (see p070). To the east is the newly rising Docklands, which awaits the Libeskind-designed Grand Canal Theatre, due for completion in 2009, the Lord Foster-designed U2 Tower, slated for 2011, and several further public spaces. Time will tell whether it will all really take off.

For full addresses, see Resources.

Four Courts
The work of acclaimed neoclassical
architect James Gandon, the Four
Courts, completed in 1802, is still home
to Ireland's Supreme Court. Gandon
incorporated Sir Christopher Wren's
stone drum from St Paul's Cathedral
into his design but with a shallow
roof akin to that on Rome's Pantheon.
The sculptures are by Edward Smyth.
Inns Quay, T 872 5555

Dublin Castle

Site of the original Dubh Linn (Black Pool), the long-gone harbour that gave the city its name, Dublin Castle was a Gaelic ringfort, a Viking military base and a Norman motte-and-bailey fortress before the English King John had a proper stone castle built in the 13th century. For the next seven centuries, it was the much-rebuilt HQ of British rule and home to a succession of lord lieutenants and viceroys. The castle played its part in the 1916 Easter Rising, being the site of the first fatality and the place where the Irish Citizen Army leader James Connolly was held until he was shot. Now it is mainly a heritage site. The castle gardens house the fascinating Chester Beatty Library (see p037).
Cork Hill, T 645 8813, dublincastle.ie

The Spire

By the 1980s, Ireland's historic main drag, O'Connell Street, had become a shabby thoroughfare of fast-food joints. In 2002, a masterplan for the area's rejuvenation was implemented, which included placing Ian Ritchie Architects' stainless-steel needle in front of the GPO (overleaf). Currently the world's tallest sculpture, The Spire – which is 3m wide at the bottom and reaches 120m high in a narrowing cone shape – can sway by up to 1.5m at the top if the wind gets up. As the light alters during the day, its reflectivity changes: now you see it, now you don't. At night, it is illuminated from the bottom and a light emerges from its tip.
O'Connell Street/Henry Street

Custom House

This neoclassical pile of Portland stone was designed by James Gandon. A pupil of the great Palladian Sir William Chambers, he was brought to Dublin from England by Wide Streets Commissioner John Beresford. Custom House, which took 10 years to build (1781-1791), was torched by the IRA in 1921 during the Civil War, and the interior and dome were destroyed. The dome was rebuilt using Ardbraccan limestone, which has a fine, white grain that takes on a grey tinge as it ages, and explains why it is much darker than the rest of the building. Gandon gave Custom House four different, ornate façades and an exterior lined with sculptures, coats of arms and carved keystones. It's now home to the Irish Department of the Environment, Heritage and Local Government.
Custom House Quay, T 888 2000

GPO

Francis Johnston's 1814 General Post Office (GPO) is fronted by a huge Ionic portico spanning five bays midway along O'Connell Street, although this is pretty much all that remains of the original building. The rest, including the great postal hall with its mezzanine level and coffered ceiling, was rebuilt after it was shelled by the British during the 1916 Easter Rising. The symbolic heart of Irish nationalism, this is where Pádraig Pearse, a member of the Irish Volunteers, read out the Proclamation of the Irish Republic. The rebels barricaded inside were never able to return effective fire against the British, but it was defeat, and the execution of 15 republican leaders, that brought Irish public opinion on their side and laid the ground for the War of Independence.

O'Connell Street

HOTELS

WHERE TO STAY AND WHICH ROOMS TO BOOK

There has been an explosion of new hotels in Dublin over the past decade, partly to cater for the hordes of visitors who continue to flow into the city for the craic, and also to serve all those software designers, property barons, rock stars and business behemoths who came for a ride on the Celtic Tiger's tail. So contemporary design nous, luxurious linens, hip bars and chichi eateries have now been added to the city's tradition of excellent service.

In some hotels, this has been achieved with greater success than in others. Taking over Sam Stephenson's modernist mews to create Number 31 (opposite) was inspired and should make the hotel a must-stay for architecture aficionados. Equally, The Morrison (see p020) is a grown-up design hotel of muted tones and sober shades. The Dylan (see p024) and The Morgan (overleaf) on the other hand might be (whisper it) just a little young and a little bling, but they certainly make a statement and make you feel like a star. At the very top of the top end, The Shelbourne (see p026), with its Princess Grace Suite dedicated to Ms Kelly, The Merrion (see p022), with its Irish art collection, and The Fitzwilliam (see p027) all deliver what they should – with seamless efficiency, attention to detail and unbeatable locations. The Shelbourne, mainly for its place in the hearts of Dubliners and its historical significance, takes first prize – but there's not much in it.

For full addresses and room rates, see Resources.

Dear Reader, books by Phaidon are recognized worldwide for their beauty, scholarship and elegance. We invite you to return this card with your name and e-mail address so that we can keep you informed of our new publications, special offers and events. Alternatively, visit us at **www.phaidon.com** to see our entire list of books, videos and stationery. Register on-line to be included on our regular e-newsletters.

Subjects in which I have a special interest

☐ General Non-Fiction   ☐ Art   ☐ Photography   ☐ Architecture   ☐ Design

☐ Fashion   ☐ Music   ☐ Children's   ☐ Food   ☐ Travel

	Mr/Miss/Ms	Initial	Surname
Name			
No./Street			
City			
Postcode/Zip code		Country	
E-mail			

This is not an order form. To order please contact Customer Services at the appropriate address overleaf.

Please delete address not required before mailing

PHAIDON PRESS LIMITED

Regent's Wharf

All Saints Street

London N1 9PA

UK

PHAIDON PRESS INC.

180 Varick Street

New York

NY 10014

USA

Return address for USA and Canada only

Return address for UK and countries
outside the USA and Canada only

Number 31

In 1958, Sam Stephenson paid £1,000 for a mews building in Leeson Close. Before Stephenson famously befriended Ireland's political élite – the architect joked that he shared a bed with Charles Haughey twice – he and two labourers transformed the interior of this period property into a gorgeous modernist space, complete with white mosaic tiling and a sunken, rectangular lounge area. In the 1960s, the mews was the centre of a swinging, high-society party scene. Now, the mews and its adjoining Georgian townhouse comprise the boutique hotel Number 31, run in relaxed style by Neil Comer and his wife, Ann. The hotel has 21 en-suite rooms, such as the Superior Double (above), and a reputation for one of the best 'full Irish' breakfasts in the city.
31 Leeson Close, T 676 5011, number31.ie

The Morgan

A self-conscious design aesthetic grips The Morgan, which boasts Verner Panton chairs, Arco floor lamps and camp chandeliers. The hotel is the work of Design Farm's Brian McDonald for the hotelier Paul Fitzpatrick. For its opulence, book the King Deluxe 228 (pictured). Soundproof glass ensures tranquil views.
10 Fleet Street, T 643 7000, themorgan.com

The Morrison

When it opened in June 1999, The Morrison created the kind of celebrity buzz design hotels like to create. Fashion designer John Rocha was the overall consultant, and he added a melange of Asian/Irish influences to architect Hugh Wallace's large, clean-lined spaces. The Asian feel comes from the combination of dark brown oak and white walls that gives the place a sense of calm. Irish notes are expressed in the abstract, Liffey-influenced form of the long carpet that runs from the riverfront door past the Café and Morrison Bars to the reception area, and the collage paintings by Irish artist Clea van der Grijn. The rooms are also subtle, not shouty, like some hotels we could mention. Try to book the Penthouse Suite (above and right) or one of the 14 rooms with river views.
Ormond Quay, T 887 2400,
www.morrisonhotel.ie

The Merrion

The most luxurious hotel in Dublin, The Merrion, is a tale of money. Sited in four converted Georgian townhouses, it is a joint venture between Billy Hastings, the former chairman of Allied Irish Banks, Lochlann Quinn and Martin Naughton, owner of global giant Glen Dimplex. Quinn and Naughton were investors in the Michelin-starred Restaurant Patrick Guilbaud (see p051) and relocated it to The Merrion. An outstanding collection of 19th- and 20th-century Irish art, including works by Nathaniel Hone, Sir John Lavery and Jack B Yeats, adorns the walls. There's a fine guests- and members-only spa and the Cellar Bar is the place to compare notes on Bentley Continentals with local Euromillionaires. Try the Junior Suite King (pictured) for a taste of the high life.

21 Merrion Street Upper, T 603 0600, merrionhotel.com

The Dylan
Housed in a converted nurses' block,
The Dylan is not about understatement,
which you'll gather as soon as you enter
the lobby (pictured). The pewter bar,
all padded stools and bold wallpaper,
attracts the yummy mummies of the
neighbourhood, who come for cocktails
and the buzz. Room 101, with its huge
bay window, is the best reservation.
Eastmoreland Place, T 660 3000, dylan.ie

The Shelbourne

The venue for the drafting of the Irish Constitution in 1922 and Grace Kelly's pied-à-terre when she was in town, The Shelbourne is a high-class establishment, complete with marble bathrooms, heavy drapes, 300-thread Carmignani cotton and beds you could hide a taxi in. Locals are fiercely possessive of the Grand Old Lady of the Green, which reopened in 2007 after a two-year renovation, with new interiors designed by Frank Nicholson. The Ice Queen of Monaco used to make do with a suite of two bedrooms and a separate dining and living area, now called the Princess Grace (above). A Deluxe may suit smaller pockets. The location is ideal and come Friday night you'll be ahead of the queue for cocktails in the No 27 Bar. *27 St Stephen's Green, T 663 4500, marriott.com*

The Fitzwilliam

Built on the site of a 1930s cinema, this was Dublin's first design hotel when it opened in 1998. Terence Conran's CD Partnership gave the hotel a lobby (above) of Spanish marble, a chrome overhead walkway and a chequered floor that some bright spark labelled 'modern baronial'. Elsewhere, this style translates as angular fireplaces, a palette of grey and lime-green and contemporary furniture by Irish siblings Tadhg and Simon O'Driscoll. The rooms are more subdued and some updating began in late 2007. Opt for one of the Superior Rooms, which are well proportioned, sleek and comfy, and have fabulous views over St Stephen's Green. The independently run, Michelin-starred restaurant Thornton's (see p057) is an absolute must for dinner. *St Stephen's Green, T 478 7000, fitzwilliamhotel.com*

The Clarence
The Arts and Crafts interior of this 1852 building was tastefully remodelled when taken over by Bono and The Edge in the 1990s. However, Foster + Partners plan to rip it up and add a glass roof in 2009, so see The Clarence now. The Penthouse Suite (pictured) is the swank booking and The Octagon Bar is an institution.
6-8 Wellington Quay, T 407 0800, theclarence.ie

Grafton House

This chic and cheerful B&B is run by Dublin's ubiquitous Eoin Foyle and Jay Bourke, who own Odessa (see p054) and Eden (see p036), among several other ventures. It provides an affordable slice of quality design in a great location in the heart of the city's clubland and is convenient for those who like to stay up late – but who don't fancy being corralled with the hen parties in Temple Bar. Ask for a room at the rear if you want to avoid street noise; our favourite is Room 14 (above). If there is a group of you, the six-berth Penthouse Apartment is the classiest way to do Dublin en masse. *26-27 South Great George's Street, T 679 2041, graftonguesthouse.com*

24 HOURS

SEE THE BEST OF THE CITY IN JUST ONE DAY

Choosing the highlights of a culturally jam-packed city like Dublin isn't easy, and clearly fans of impenetrable modernist tomes will decry our lack of Joycean connections. You could, of course, rectify this by squeezing in a trip to the James Joyce Centre (35 North Great George's Street, T 878 8547), or if your 24 hours happens to fall on 16 June, by taking part in the annual Bloomsday high jinks; but we think you would be better off actually reading *Ulysses*, rather than just trooping into Davy Byrnes (21 Duke Street, T 677 5217) for a gorgonzola sandwich and a glass of burgundy.

There will also be nationalist history buffs who can't believe we've left Kilmainham Gaol (Inchicore Road, T 453 5984) and the heroic story of Countess Markievicz and the other paragons of 1916 off our itinerary. And they could have a point, but time is a consideration, and the jail's guided tour needs several hours to do it justice. Nevertheless, we do think the combination of ethical cuisine at Nude (opposite), modern art at the Hugh Lane Gallery (overleaf), a contemporary Irish lunch at Eden (see p036) and stand-up comedy at The International Bar (see p038), leavened with some ancient manuscripts at the Chester Beatty Library (see p037) and a Dublin institution, the Trocadero (4 St Andrew Street, T 677 5545), for a late-night supper, offers a quirky and original slice of the city that can't be bettered.

For full addresses, see Resources.

09.00 Nude

There are numerous places in the city that serve a full Irish breakfast – bacon, eggs, white pudding, soda bread and boxty (potato pancake) – including hotel Number 31 (see p017) and The Mermaid Café (see p041). But for those who like their arteries less clogged, Nude is a chainette of healthy eateries owned by Bono's brother, Norman Hewson. Lime-green in décor and very green in ethical outlook, the food and juices are organically produced, free range, locally sourced where possible, preservative-free, freshly made and all the other high-minded things that you would expect of the Hewson family. We think that a breakfast of Fairtrade coffee, wheatgrass juice, muesli and freshly baked bread is a very Ireland-of-the-moment way to start your day. *21 Suffolk Street, T 677 4804, nude.ie*

10.30 Hugh Lane Gallery
This is probably one of the best collections
of modern and contemporary art in
Ireland, boasting major works by Manet,
Degas and Renoir. Its acquisition in 1998
of Baggot Street-born Francis Bacon's
entire studio – slashed canvases, artist's
materials and all – has made for a superb
permanent exhibition (pictured).
Charlemont House, Parnell Square North,
T 222 5550, hughlane.ie

13.00 Eden

Part of the Eoin Foyle and Jay Bourke empire, Eden is a feast for the eyes and the tastebuds. It was designed in 1997 in an eclectic modern style by Tom de Paor. He put up a mosaic wall, mingled Swedish Johanson Design furniture with old wooden pieces and draped hanging plants down the rough concrete, double-height pillars. Eden has a terrace overlooking Meeting House Square, and in summer you can watch a movie projected onto a wall of the Gallery of Photography (see p066) from your table. You might also want to devote your attention to the food, which is high-quality modern Irish with a twist. Wallpaper* will be going back for chef Michael Durkin's roast fillet of cod with chive mash and hazelnut and dill butter. *Meeting House Square, T 670 5372, edenrestaurant.ie*

15.00 Chester Beatty Library

Sir Alfred Chester Beatty was a successful New York-born, Irish-naturalised mining baron who ploughed his wealth into what is probably the finest collection of manuscripts and books amassed by an amateur enthusiast in the 20th century. Housed in this purpose-built extension to Dublin Castle's Clock Tower Building, its treasures include the earliest sources on papyrus for the Bible, dating from the 2nd to the 4th century AD, including copies of the four Gospels and Acts of the Apostles, the Letters of St Paul and various Old Testament fragments. The beautiful Islamic Collection includes 260 Qur'ans, many dating from the late 8th and 9th centuries, while the East Asian Collection has the largest assortment of jade books from the Imperial Court outside China. *Dublin Castle, Cork Hill, T 407 0750, cbl.ie*

20.00 The International Bar

Unfazed by the increasing popularity of its neighbourhood, this old-school boozer continues to serve pints to a mixed crowd of suits, students, hipsters and tourists, just as it has for years. Many of them come for the legendary comedy club upstairs, open four nights a week. The birthplace of virtually every Irish comic to grace British TV schedules over the last two decades, it has witnessed the debuts of everyone from Dylan Moran to Dara O'Briain, and impromptu guest spots from the likes of Eddie Izzard. After the show, go for a late supper of steak and red wine at theatrical hangout the Trocadero (T 677 5545). It may not have a Michelin star, but it's cosy as a cardi, as camp as a row of tents and a fabulous place to end a great day.
25 Wicklow Street, T 677 9250, international-bar.com

URBAN LIFE
CAFÉS, RESTAURANTS, BARS AND NIGHTCLUBS

Affluence has brought a new-found appreciation of food to Ireland and a raft of top-notch restaurants to service its new connoisseurs. For a city of its size, Dublin has an impressive number of Michelin stars and boasts several eateries on the cusp of recognition. Many of these are located in the ritzier hotels, and making a reservation before you hit town is a must at the top end. The combination of high-quality local produce and friendly service makes dining out here a relaxed, unstuffy pleasure at any level.

There is also fun to be had, famously, by taking part in Dublin's energetic nightlife. Despite its reputation, Temple Bar does have the odd civilised nook, such as Eden (see p036), the bar at The Morgan (see p018) or the insider's secret that is the unpretentious cellar trattoria Il Baccaro (Meeting House Square, T 671 4597). The locals' main going-out areas tend to be sandwiched between Grafton Street and South Great George's Street, and around Merrion Row. Classic wood-lined Victorian pubs that never gave way to the superpub trend have been rediscovered, if they ever really went out of fashion, by all classes and all ages. We highlight a few of the best here, but could have added The Long Hall (51 South Great George's Street, T 475 1590), The Stag's Head (1 Dame Court, T 679 3687) and Grogan's (15 William Street South, T 677 9320) – all of them warm, convivial refuges from the world. *For full addresses, see Resources.*

The Mermaid Café

Chef-restaurateur Ben Gorman has been serving up big flavours with his robust, bistro-style food in this informal and light-filled corner restaurant since 1996. His menus are decidedly transatlantic, with a kind of France-meets-Maine feel to them. Dishes include cassoulet and New England crab cakes, homemade *saucisson* and pecan pie. The décor is plain, and features bare floorboards, rustic tables, abstract art and an open kitchen. Two large windows look out over busy Dame Street, and the restaurant also runs a delicatessen next door. At lunch and dinner, the crowd is mixed, from pinstriped to ponytailed, while brunch at The Mermaid is a relaxed, atmospheric and chatty way to spend a Sunday morning. *69-70 Dame Street, T 670 8236, mermaid.ie*

Bang Café

The owners of Bang Café, brothers Simon and Christian Stokes, come from foodie-fashionista stock. Their father, Jeff, co-owns long-time power-lunch institution Unicorn (T 676 2182), while their Danish-born mother, Pia Bang, runs a luxurious, eponymous interiors and accessories store (T 888 3777). Bang Café is a modern, stylish bar and restaurant spread over three floors in an airy building located at the heart of Georgian Dublin's going-out street. Popular with lunching yummy mummies and a thirtysomething evening crowd, the restaurant sources from Irish producers where possible and makes a point of listing its suppliers. The bangers with chive mash and mustard shallot jus is, naturally, the signature dish.
11 Merrion Row, T 676 0898,
bangrestaurant.com

L'Ecrivain

Chef-owner Derry Clarke grew up
in a family of food traders and worked
at Dublin's legendary Le Coq Hardi before
opening L'Ecrivain in 1989, which has
since won a Michelin star. The menu
is French-Irish, often very Irish – black
pudding and pig's feet have made
an appearance – and game-tinged, with
pigeon, quail, duck and venison served
up regularly. It's not a showy place, and
occupies a low-key upstairs room.
However, it is a venue where celebrity
patrons know they'll make the gossip
columns if they show up together and
giggle conspiratorially. Book weekend
reservations at least three weeks ahead.
*109 Baggot Street Lower, T 661 1919,
lecrivain.com*

List for Beer, Sherry, Sparkling & Dessert Wine's, thanks ✳

ROSÉ

• Enate rosado '06
  Cabernet Sauvignon
  SPAIN €5.45
• Castello di Ama '06
  Sangiorese, ITALY
  €6.30
• Murolo Jester '07
  Sangiorese
  mclarenvale, AUS
  €8-

THE GLASS

RED

• Villa Tonino 05 Nero d'...
  Sicily, ITALY €6
• Bodega Lurton 06 Malbec
  Mendoza, ARGENTINA €...
• Saint Joseph les challey...
  Syrah -Rhône, FRANCE ...
• Firesteed 05 Pinot noir
  Oregon, USA €8
• Riccitelli estate '04 cabernet
  Mendoza, ARGENTINA €10
• Sanchez '04 tempranillo
  Ribera del Duero SPAIN €11

The Winding Stair

Taking its name from a collection of WB Yeats poetry, The Winding Stair café and bookshop became a hangout for arty types in the 1970s, when the city was lacking in alternative venues. Its big windows and riverside location, right by the Ha'penny Bridge, make it a sentimental haunt for those old enough to remember a time before everyone in Ireland was a property millionaire. There was dismay when

it closed in 2005, but it was rescued by the Thomas Read Group, which owns several venues in town. On the ground floor, the bookshop sells new and second-hand books, while upstairs, chef Áine Maguire serves excellent modern Irish food, such as corned beef with crispy cabbage, horseradish mash and mustard sauce.
40 Ormond Quay, T 872 7320, www.winding-stair.com

Locks

Located on the Grand Canal in Portobello, Locks had been a grande dame of the Dublin scene for 26 years before it changed hands in 2006. It was taken over by husband-and-wife owners Kelvin Rynhart and Teresa Carr. Rynhart used to work at Bang Café (see p042), while Carr managed the restaurant at La Stampa Hotel (T 677 4444). They brought in designer Simon Walker, who created a stylish, comfortable interior, and hotshot chef Troy Maguire, who had made a name for himself at L'Gueuleton (see p062). At Locks, he produces hearty but high-quality, bistro-luxe dishes, including starters such as black pudding and apple *tarte tatin*, and mains with lots of meat and pulses. You can also drop in for an hors d'œuvre platter with wine. *1 Windsor Terrace, T 454 3391, locksrestaurant.ie*

Bewley's Oriental Café

The Bewley family has been selling tea and coffee to the Irish since 1835. Their flagship is a huge, three-storey café, which even has its own theatre, on Dublin's main shopping drag. It is as integral to local life as Trinity College, which supplies much of its staff and customers, but its existence is threatened by the ever-rising rents on Grafton Street. After years of declining standards, it closed briefly in 2004, before being rescued by Eoin Foyle and Jay Bourke, who gave it a sympathetic revamp on the ground floor, where six important art nouveau stained-glass windows by Harry Clarke have been back-lit to make them more visible. It makes a much more interesting java pit stop than any of the chains in town. *78-79 Grafton Street, T 672 7720, bewleyscafe.com*

Fallon & Byrne

This four-storey foodie emporium was created from an impressive 1920 warehouse located in the heart of the going-out district to the west of Grafton Street. It has all the varieties of smoked paprika and arborio rice you could want in the main food hall, and the bistro-style restaurant gets good reviews, though we were drawn to the basement (above). This houses a spacious wine cellar and tapas-style bar, serving a mix of Irish and Mediterranean nibbles, from oysters to marinated fungi, complemented by an extensive wine list. The whole building was stylishly refurbished with input from the co-proprietor Paul Byrne, who brought the idea back with him after a stint living in Manhattan.
11-17 Exchequer Street, T 472 1000, fallonandbyrne.com

The Horseshoe Bar

The Constitution Room in The Shelbourne might well have seen Michael Collins in founding-father mode, but the hotel's Horseshoe Bar is where Brendan Behan spent his earnings from *Borstal Boy* (well, some of them – Behan was hardly a selective drinker). It traditionally had a louche reputation – one Dublin wit memorably characterised it as the place where 'women with a past met men with no future' – and a devoted following of media-legal-politico types. During the two-year refit of The Shelbourne, Sam Stephenson's original 1957 interior was sympathetically restored, and while the glamour pusses hit the hotel's No 27 Bar and Lounge, the windowless Horseshoe remains a proper drinker's refuge. *The Shelbourne, 27 St Stephen's Green North, T 663 4500, marriott.com*

Restaurant Patrick Guilbaud

Ever since he opened his first Dublin restaurant in the early 1980s, Normandy native Patrick Guilbaud has been serving sublime Frenchified fare using the best of Ireland's produce. Head chef Guillaume Lebrun, who has worked with Guilbaud for more than 20 years, has a firm lock on Ireland's only two-Michelin-starred restaurant, with signature dishes such as Clogher Head lobster ravioli made with coconut-scented lobster cream, handmade pasta, toasted almonds and flavoured olive oil. The restaurant is housed in an airy part of The Merrion Hotel (see p022), with large windows overlooking gardens designed by landscape artist Jim Reynolds. The tables are big and well spaced, and your bill is likely to be equally impressive.
21 Upper Merrion Street, T 676 4192, restaurantpatrickguilbaud.ie

Kehoe's

After the gastropub boom of the 1990s, the young are falling in love with Dublin's old boozers again, and the splendid Kehoe's, off Grafton Street, is particularly cherished. Filled with nooks and crannies, it has been a pub for 200 years and was owned by the Kehoe family from 1903 until 1996, when John Kehoe, who lived upstairs, sold out for a record £1.96m. Fortunately, the new owners left it untouched, except for turning the upstairs into a lounge. The tiny snug at the front has its own door to the street, so that once upon a time women and priests could get in for a drink unseen, and there are other teeny rooms off the main bar. Kehoe's attracts a diverse crowd, from hipsters to old men, and you will find yourself coming back again and again.

9 Anne Street South, T 677 8312

Tea Room

This historic fine-dining restaurant in The Clarence (see p028) is quite simply one of the most delightful Dublin spots in which to sit and eat. Lofty ceilings, lots of oak and huge windows create a timeless charm that may not survive Foster + Partners' plans for redeveloping the boutique hotel. Young executive chef Mathieu Melin has been working in Michelin-starred restaurants since he was 15 – and it shows.

His chicken and foie gras terrine with pear and apple chutney and walnut and raisin bread is a winner, as is his great-value Market Menu – a high-end special available at lunch, all night Sunday to Thursday, and for early-bird dinners at the weekend. *The Clarence, 6-8 Wellington Quay, T 407 0813, theclarence.ie*

Odessa

Designed by co-owner Peter O'Kennedy, white-hot Odessa is a restaurant with a members' lounge and club above. But this being Ireland, it is nothing like as snooty as similar ventures in London. The place starts to fill up with media, design and fashion folk after 11pm, and if they get cold on the smoking balcony, there is a pile of Puffa jackets to share.
14 Dame Court, T 670 7634

Anseo

This little bit of Shoreditch across the sea was once Con's Pub, a simple old man's bolt-hole that never made it onto the tourist trail. Then in came new owners, some blacked-out windows, low-level lighting, quality DJs and the increasingly necessary Irish name. There followed lots of web designers with trendy specs, undiscovered artists and legions of beautiful young things. It can get a mite sweaty on a Saturday night for somewhere so relentlessly cool, but at least you'll make friends. The music hops around, from funk to groove and Afro-beat to Kraftwerk and Dolly Parton. And to think there are people still in their thirties who remember that nightclubbing in Dublin once meant wearing a jacket and tie to an over-priced cellar in Leeson Street.
18 Camden Street Lower, T 475 1321

Thornton's

Dublin chef Kevin Thornton gets as many
headlines for his feuds as for his food.
Which is a pity, because his cooking is very
good. Decidedly high-end – he did have
two Michelin stars, but is back down to one
– his is delicate, subtle fare, but no less
innovative for it. Thornton seems to have
taken some of the fuss out of his dishes
since losing a star and brought in New
York designer David Piscuskas and his firm,
1100: Architect, to make over the
restaurant in response to complaints that
it felt too 'cold'. Thornton's reputation for
having a hot temper is overdone, but don't,
under any circumstances, order chips that
aren't on the menu and then send them
back to the kitchen, as one diner did. He
will call you names and *will* throw you out.
*Fitzwilliam Hotel, 128 St Stephen's Green,
T 478 7008, fitzwilliamhotel.com*

Hogan's

This place has good claim to be Dublin's first superpub. When Declan O'Regan opened Hogan's in 1992, he tried to find an espresso machine and was told there would be no market for a Continental-style café/bar in Dublin. But his laid-back bar and basement (with DJs) has been so successful that he has expanded into the restaurant trade with a bistro, L'Gueuleton (see p062), next door. Hogan's has a late licence, and attracts a mixed crowd of twenty- and thirtysomethings who drop in for a final boogie before calling it quits. It also makes a relaxing hangout for a Sunday wind-down. The big windows looking out over the street give it a much more open feel than many trad pubs.
35 South Great George's Street, T 677 5904

Doheny & Nesbitt

Some say that the Celtic Tiger wasn't planned and executed by deals in plush restaurants, but over pints of Guinness between politicians and developers in Doheny & Nesbitt. Just around the corner from Leinster House, home of the Irish Parliament, or Dáil, it has long been a haunt and meeting place for TDs, or members of the Dáil, and political correspondents looking for a story.

Fianna Fáil, Ireland's dominant political party, holds its annual Christmas shindig for hacks upstairs, so the Prime Minister is not an unusual sight. Thursday and Friday nights see a big, mixed crowd, not all of them politicos in bad suits. Conversations are easily struck up and the atmosphere does ooze a certain indefinable sense of being in the thick of things.

4-5 Baggot Street Lower, T 676 2945

Krystle

Despite a name that reminds us of a certain vintage soap, Krystle is a bona fide nightclubbing hit, especially if you are a twentysomething rich kid who went to one of Dublin's fee-paying schools. This is also the place to find that wannabe model who will look so good on the pale grey passenger seat of your Audi TT. While visiting international celebrities seem to hit the institution that is Lillies Bordello (T 679 9204), sports stars, soap princesses and a fairly wide swathe of the young end of the Dublin 4 postcode will make it to Krystle between Thursday and Saturday, thanks in the main to under-30 promoters Brian O'Malley and Conor Buckley. The place is decorated in a pale, creamy style, sort of minimalism meets bling, which, come to think of it, is a good description of the way its female customers dress.
*21-25 Harcourt Street, T 478 4066,
krystlenightclub.com*

INSIDER'S GUIDE

MARIA MACVEIGH, ARCHITECT AND INTERIOR DESIGNER

An award-winning architect and interior designer, Maria MacVeigh lives on the Grand Canal in Georgian Dublin. She has a studio in the centre of town, opposite Trinity College, and teaches design at the Dublin Institute of Technology. For a midweek lunch, she recommends Fallon & Byrne (see p048) or Lara Lu Foods (1 George's Street Arcade, T 087 990 8003), where she meets her cousins for some falafel or soup at the bar and 'the best coffee in Dublin'. On Saturday, she often has brunch at Eden (see p036), which she likes for its beautiful, double-height room, designed by Tom de Paor, friendly staff and unfussy food. In the evening, MacVeigh heads to Chapter One (18-19 Parnell Square, T 873 2266) for a pre-theatre meal – the best time to get a booking.

Another spot she enjoys immensely is L'Gueuleton (1 Fade Street, T 675 3708). 'Get there at six, put your name down and busy yourself with a pint in The Long Hall (see p040) across the street until you are called over for dinner. My favourite way of dining there is to sit at the bar with a friend and order a plate of grilled Irish oysters and Guinness brown bread.' Many of MacVeigh's favourite places have remained unchanged by the city's sudden affluence, such as the lounge at The Clarence (see p028), with its Arts and Crafts panelling, and the smallest pub in Ireland, Dawson Lounge (25 Dawson Street, T 671 0311).

For full addresses, see Resources.

ARCHITOUR

A GUIDE TO DUBLIN'S ICONIC BUILDINGS

Some wags will tell you that Dublin doesn't do modernism, only rain, Catholic guilt and Georgian houses. And there's no doubt a proportion of the city wishes that, architecturally, that were true.

Many great controversies raged in the 1960s and 1970s around the city's modern developments – especially the 1975 Electricity Supply Board HQ (Fitzwilliam Street), which replaced a chunk of the Georgian Mile with a building by the great bête noire of the heritage lobby, Sam Stephenson. And yet the 30-years-to-be-appreciated rule seems to apply. The incongruity of the Central Bank of Ireland (see p070) on the edge of low-rise Temple Bar hasn't diminished, but the building has slowly won acceptance from the public, thanks to the sheer drama of its bulk, while Michael Scott's bus station, Busáras (p068), is rightly appreciated as a landmark of postwar European design. Modernists should also thank the enlightened chancellors of Trinity College, who have repeatedly turned to the architectural cutting edge when in need of extra library space (see p072 and p074).

The boom years have produced mainly bland apartment blocks, with just a few notable exceptions, such as Alto Vetro (opposite) and the Department of Finance extension (see p076). Meanwhile, the jury is still out on the contributions that are currently being made to the Docklands by a wave of showy architects.

For full addresses, see Resources.

Alto Vetro

There are lots of uninspired residential buildings in the redevelopment area to the east of the city centre. Height limitations have produced serried ranks of chunky apartment blocks and even landscape architect Martha Schwartz's Grand Canal Square is a little windswept and soulless. The area may improve with the completion of Daniel Libeskind's Grand Canal Theatre in 2009 and a hotel by Manuel Aires Mateus. But until then, the best building in the docks is Shay Cleary's sleek Alto Vetro: 16 storeys of modern living space that arrived in 2007 for the Celtic Tiger's most exhibitionistic and monied inhabitants. The design makes the most of its small footprint, its slim glass tower breaking free of the monotonous roof line of the canal basin area.
Grand Canal Quay

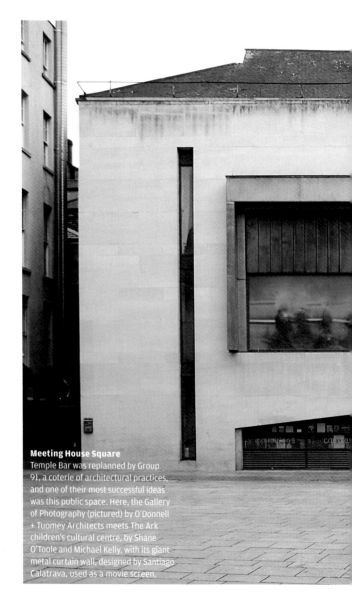

Meeting House Square
Temple Bar was replanned by Group
91, a coterie of architectural practices,
and one of their most successful ideas
was this public space. Here, the Gallery
of Photography (pictured) by O'Donnell
+ Tuomey Architects meets The Ark
children's cultural centre, by Shane
O'Toole and Michael Kelly, with its giant
metal curtain wall, designed by Santiago
Calatrava, used as a movie screen.

Busáras

Quite simply Ireland's most important 20th-century building, this iconic bus station, designed by Michael Scott, also has claims to international fame. Completed in 1953, it was one of the first major modernist buildings erected in Europe after WWII; it was Ove Arup's first international engineering commission; and it used Le Corbusier's Modulor system of proportions, which dictated the location of the concrete fins between the glazing and the position of the wave-form canopy. It's also one of the few examples of integrated building design in Ireland – Scott and his team, Michael Scott Architects, were responsible for the interior, including furniture, door handles and light fittings. It once housed a cinema, restaurant and there were plans for a nightclub.
Store Street

Central Bank of Ireland
This controversial hulk of a building was
designed by Stephenson Gibney and
Associates in the late 1960s, when Temple
Bar was a rundown dock area earmarked
for replacement with a bus station. The
tall, strikingly horizontal office block with
a strict geometric form, its floors hanging
from exposed steel struts, went up in
1978. The bus station never arrived.
Dame Street

Berkeley Library

In commissioning this brutalist gem, the elders of Trinity College displayed remarkable bravery and vision. In 1960, apart from Busáras (see p068), there were virtually no other modern buildings in the very Georgian Dublin, and to step into Trinity was to step into the past; a place of 18th- and 19th-century squares. Ahrends Behrends Koralek's building sits in an elevated position, because of the book vault underneath, right next to Thomas Burgh's Old Library, which houses the much-visited Book of Kells. With its Douglas Fir imprints in the reinforced concrete walls and its boxy monumentalism, the library doesn't take any prisoners. And yet it has been popular since it opened in 1967 for, among other things, the indirect light created by the unusual curved windows.
Trinity College

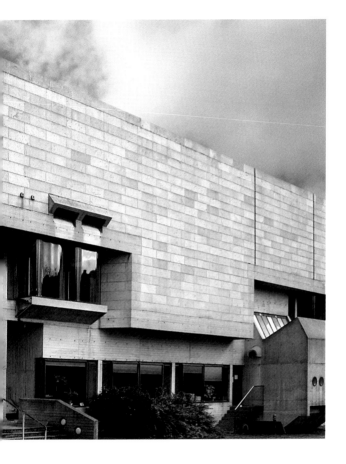

James Ussher Library
Tucked in a small plot between two buildings by Ahrends Behrends Koralek, McCullough-Mulvin Architects and KMD Architecture's sleek, sometimes austere, 2002 library has provided an answer to its location. Its three linked blocks — the 'tower of books', a tall, slice-of-glass atrium and the main glass-fronted reading rooms — rise from a platform.
Trinity College

Department of Finance
This 2008 addition to the Department
of Finance is so lovely, it is almost
kissable. This is warm, human-scale
architecture wrapped up in tactile
Ballinasloe limestone. Connected to
the existing complex, it occupies a
prominent position just off St Stephen's
Green and beside the historic Huguenot
cemetery. Most Irish government
departments are housed in old colonial
buildings and this is the first purpose-
built headquarters since the Department
of Industry and Commerce on Kildare
Street was put up in 1942. Someone in
the Office of Public Works has taste and
should be promoted for choosing this
welcoming, solid, but not hefty design
by Shelley McNamara and Yvonne
Farrell of Grafton Architects.
Merrion Row, T 676 7571

Bank of Ireland HQ
With its bronze manganese curtain walls — the same material used in NYC's Seagram Building — lack of detailing and simple proportions, it's obvious that architect Ronald Tallon drew on his time as a student of Mies van der Rohe. The 1978 HQ comprises three buildings, the tallest of which is eight storeys, so it sneaks a tower block into the cityscape.
50-55 Lower Baggot Street

SHOPPING

THE BEST RETAIL THERAPY AND WHAT TO BUY

Like many small countries, Ireland doesn't support an extensive contemporary furniture and product design industry, but notable makers include Simon and Tadhg O'Driscoll (opposite) and Kate Fine (see p084), both of whom often work to commission. For Irish decorative arts, the once government-run shop Kilkenny (6 Nassau Street, T 677 7066) stocks some important designers, such as the world-renowned potters Louis Mulcahy and Stephen Pearce. Another essential artisanal stop-off is Sheridans Cheesemongers (11 Anne Street South, T 679 3143), where Kevin and Seamus Sheridan lay claim to Ireland's best cheese selection.

Dublin's fashion scene is much more vibrant, with plenty of chic boutiques to choose from at the western end of Temple Bar, including 5 Scarlet Row (overleaf), or in the lanes just off Grafton Street. Sadly, Grafton Street itself has been taken over by high-street chains, though brand temple Brown Thomas (see p086) is a must-visit. Also worth checking out are the one-of-a-kind vintage-couture boutique Jenny Vander (50 Drury Street, T 677 0406) and the absolutely peachy children's clothes store Milk + Cookies (14 Westbury Mall, T 671 0104). Among the hottest Irish designers to look out for are Joanne Hynes (T 087 993 2107), known for her dresses and tailoring, and Eilis Boyle (T 443 3268), whose pared-down knitwear has made her a success as far afield as Asia.
For full addresses, see Resources.

O'Driscoll Furniture

Brothers Simon and Tadhg O'Driscoll have been making furniture for architects, interior-design commissions and corporate clients for more than 15 years. As with anyone who is anyone in Ireland, their clients have included U2, as well as hotels such as The Morrison (see p020) and The Clarence (see p028). Now all of us can purchase a slice of the brothers' cool, Eames-influenced, contemporary furniture and accessories at their showroom just off Pearse Street. We like their zebrawood coffee table with splayed stainless-steel legs and their red 'Armitage' daybed for its clean-lined, utilitarian simplicity. *26-28 Lombard Street East, T 671 1069, oddesign.com*

5 Scarlet Row
Irish-American designer Eileen Shields
lists Eva Longoria and Halle Berry
among the devotees of her high-
concept, yet unpretentious shoe line.
This store, which she co-owns, hosts
her entire collection as well as art
exhibitions at the back of the shop, which
is run by the other owner, Vaari Claffey.
*5 Scarlet Row, Essex Street West,
T 672 9534, eileenshields.com*

Fine Design

Artist and designer Kate Fine produces
innovative and attractive furniture,
mirror installations and lighting. She
works to commission, preferring her
clients – architects, interior designers
and, increasingly, private individuals
– to specify dimensions, shape and
finish before she comes up with a final
blueprint. We particularly like her series
of occasional tables inspired by vintage
wallpaper (left), from £655, and featuring
a reworked classic damask motif etched
onto mirrored sheets wrapped around
the frame. She has also produced back-lit,
mirrored light boxes using the same
pattern, as well as a recent range called
Mirrored Art, in which the work of local
artists is etched onto wall mirrors.
*Unit 34, The Design Tower, Grand Canal
Quay, T 670 3699, finedesign.ie*

Brown Thomas
A Grafton Street institution since 1849,
Dublin's grande-dame department store
is the place to check out the collections
of the big Irish designers, such as Paul
Costelloe, Lainey Keogh and Louise
Kennedy. And those with Imelda-esque
tendencies can get their Jimmy Choo fix
in the extensively stocked Shoe Rooms.
*88-95 Grafton Street, T 605 6666,
brownthomas.com*

SPORTS AND SPAS

WORK OUT, CHILL OUT OR JUST WATCH

The big name in Irish sports is the Gaelic Athletic Association, which was founded in 1884 for 'the preservation and cultivation of national pastimes'. Initially, this meant track and field events, but it quickly came to include hurling and Gaelic football. Its headquarters and main stadium, Croke Park (overleaf), holds a place in Irish history, having been the scene of the Bloody Sunday outrage of November 1920. The growth of Ireland's middle class has resulted in a real surge of interest in rugby union – once the preserve of the privately educated élite – and Ireland's annual home Six Nations matches are real festival weekends in the city.

For participatory sports – if, that is, betting on the outcome can be called participation – horse racing arouses Irish passions in a way it no longer does in the UK; watch the drama unfold at Leopardstown Racecourse (see p094). There are also half-a-dozen top-flight golf courses within an hour or so of Dublin – the country hotel Rathsallagh House (Dunlavin, County Wicklow, T 045 403 112) has one of its own and is a good base for others nearby.

The best pampering in town is to be had at the Asian-influenced Mandala Spa (see p092). Once re-energised, you have the expanse of Dublin Bay to explore: jog or swim, or enjoy the fantastic views from the Great South Wall, where half of south Dublin comes on a Sunday to promenade out to the Poolbeg Lighthouse.

For full addresses, see Resources.

National Aquatic Centre

Ireland's national swimming centre was intended to survive without government subsidy, so the dramatic, glass-roofed shed dedicated to competition swimming and diving is connected to an enormous drum-shaped building, stuffed with wave pools and water slides. London-based specialist pool and stadia design firm S&P Architects had its work cut out making the two parts look like a whole, but once you are inside, either under the giant curved roof of the main pool (above) or whooshing down the flumes, you're unlikely to care. If the weather's fine, however, nothing beats a dip in the sea at Sandycove, below the Martello Tower, to the south-east of town. *Snugborough Road, T 646 4300, nationalaquaticcentre.ie*

Croke Park Stadium

This is a behemoth of a sports ground, partly because of its capacity, which at 82,300 is one of the largest in Europe, and partly because Gaelic football and hurling require considerably larger pitches than rugby and football. Hurling is a terrifying stick-and-ball game, a bit like a combination of field hockey, lacrosse and baseball, while Gaelic football is similar to Aussie Rules, in which players can both punch and kick the ball. In 2005, the Gaelic Athletic Association, which runs Croke Park, agreed to relax its rule forbidding 'foreign' sports to be played on its pitches, and rugby and football will be hosted here until 2010, while Lansdowne Road (T 238 2300) is redeveloped into a 50,000-seater. Croke Park also hosts stadium rockers such as Bon Jovi, U2 and Elton John. *Jones's Road, T 819 2300, crokepark.ie*

Mandala Spa

Interior designer and owner Sarah
Murray enlisted the help of Portuguese
designer Miguel Câncio Martins to create
this elegant pampering palace. Located
in La Stampa Hotel, Mandala is full
of dark spaces, polished teak, mosaics,
brick and silk, and boasts a fabulous
white marble bathtub. India, China,
Japan, Thailand and Indonesia are all
represented in the staff and the treatment
menu. There is a bewildering array
of choice – including a hot herbal poultice
that was once used on returning Thai
warriors, a Javanese LuLur massage
to soften the skin and a range of traditional
Thai massages, which are believed to
restore balance and energy to the body.
Dual sessions for couples are popular.
La Stampa Hotel, 35 Dawson Street,
T 677 4444, mandala.ie

Leopardstown Racecourse
This is the closest racecourse to the
centre of Dublin. Its biggest meetings
of the year are around Christmas, when
it hosts the National Hunt festival,
but flat races are held most Wednesday
nights during the summer. There are
several good-quality cafés and bars, and
the on-course Silken Glider restaurant
has views over the parade ring.
T 289 0500, www.leopardstown.com

ESCAPES

WHERE TO GO IF YOU WANT TO LEAVE TOWN

A couple of hours out of Dublin in any direction could see you well into the heart of Ireland – or indeed out of the country altogether if you decide to take the two-hour rail trip to Belfast and sample an urban culture revived not just by economics but by peace. The much-bombed Europa (Great Victoria Street, T 00 44 28 9027 1066) is Bill Clinton's Belfast hangout of choice, or you could hit the chic Malmaison (34-38 Victoria Street, T 00 44 28 9022 0200). Unless you're actively interested, you won't know you're in a divided city.

More bucolic pursuits abound among the historic monuments of Meath or the hilly uplands of County Wicklow, Dubliners' playground – the catch being that picturesque valleys such as Glendalough become very crowded in the summer. When you're feeling indolent, the cool luxury of Bellinter House (opposite) is likely to appeal. It provides Dublin's glitterati with a country-house retreat with a knowing wink to kitsch. If you seek a more ascetic escape, the high-design havens at Clonmel (overleaf) are a far cry from the gloomy caves that used to serve as hermitages.

Even closer to the capital is the hilly peninsula of Howth, 15km north of the centre. The best reason to visit is to eat the flappingly fresh fish – the stylish eaterie Aqua (1 West Pier, T 832 0690), housed in an old yacht club on the West Pier, also has claim to one of the best restaurant views in the whole of Dublin.

For full addresses, see Resources.

Bellinter House, Navan

This austere 1750 mansion, an hour's drive from the city, was designed by Richard Cassels, who was the architect of Dublin's parliament building, Leinster House. It passed through various ascendancy families and the Sisters of Sion before being bought by the management of Eden (see p036) and Odessa (see p054). A three-year, £10m renovation overseen by architect Pierce Tynan has produced a country house with a touch of acid house. The grand Palladian rooms have club-style furniture mixed with accents of cowhide, a blue-baize pool table and flatscreen TVs. Guests can unwind in the spa, pool and games room or go clay pigeon shooting, dine in an outpost of Eden and drink at a bar complete with a David Godbold mural. *County Meath, T 046 903 0900, bellinterhouse.com*

Glencomeragh House, Clonmel

Sometimes you need a little space to contemplate life, and there is no better place than in the serene modernist embrace of the four hermitages, or *poustinia* (from the Russian for 'desert'), designed by the Dublin firm Bates Maher for Glencomeragh House, a religious community run by the Rosminian Order. Three of these retreat boxes are built on a hill overlooking the main house, on cantilevered concrete bases that shoot out into space. Inside, they are equipped with underfloor heating, simple but sleek kitchens and sleeping facilities, and a sunken bath. Each also has a glassed-off interior courtyard – or slice of courtyard (overleaf) – to allow some outside in. Clonmel is around two-and-a-half hours by car from Dublin. This is the place do some thinking inside the box.
County Tipperary, T 052 33 181, glencomeragh.ie

Hermitage, Glencomeragh House, Clonmel

The Mound of Light, County Wexford
Designed by the venerable Ronald Tallon of Scott Tallon Walker Architects as a monument to the 1798 Irish rebellion against the English, The Mound of Light, or in Gaelic, *Tulach A'Tsolais*, is a sober slice of concrete cut out of a green hill, rather like a futuristic long barrow. The passage (or slice) leads to a chamber (left) paved with granite slabs and lined with concrete panels. In the chamber are two horizontal sculptures, made from 200-year-old Irish oak, by artist Michael Warren. The peaceful setting adds to the power of this austere but affecting structure. This is a doable day trip, as it's two hours from Dublin by car, or you could choose to spend the night 20 miles away in the somewhat camp, baroque finery of the splendid Marlfield House (T 053 942 1124). *Oulart Hill, County Wexford*

NOTES

SKETCHES AND MEMOS

RESOURCES

CITY GUIDE DIRECTORY

A

Alto Vetro 065
Grand Canal Quay

Anseo 056
18 Camden Street Lower
T 475 1321

Aqua 096
1 West Pier
Howth
T 832 0690

The Ark 066
11a Eustace Street
T 670 7788
ark.ie

B

Il Baccaro 040
Meeting House Square
T 671 4597

Bang Café 042
11 Merrion Row
T 676 0898
bangrestaurant.com

Bank of Ireland HQ 078
50-55 Lower Baggot Street

Berkeley Library 072
Trinity College

Bewley's Oriental Café 047
78-79 Grafton Street
T 672 7720
bewleyscafe.com

Brown Thomas 086
88-95 Grafton Street
T 605 6666
brownthomas.com

Busáras 068
Store Street

C

Central Bank of Ireland 070
Dame Street

Chapter One 062
18-19 Parnell Square
T 873 2266
www.chapteronerestaurant.com

Chester Beatty Library 037
Dublin Castle
Cork Hill
T 407 0750
cbl.ie

Croke Park Stadium 090
Jones's Road
T 819 2300
crokepark.ie

Custom House 014
Custom House Quay
T 888 2000

D

Davy Byrnes 032
21 Duke Street
T 677 5217
davybyrnes.com

Dawson Lounge 062
25 Dawson Street
T 671 0311
dawsonlounge.ie

Department of Finance 076
Merrion Row
T 676 7571
finance.gov.ie

Department of Industry and Commerce 076
Kildare Street

Doheny & Nesbitt 059
4-5 Baggot Street Lower
T 676 2945

Dublin Castle 012
Cork Hill
T 645 8813
dublincastle.ie

E
L'Ecrivain 044
109 Baggot Street Lower
T 661 1919
lecrivan.com
Eden 036
Meeting House Square
T 670 5372
edenrestaurant.ie
Eilis Boyle 080
T 443 3268
eilisboyle.com
Electricity Supply Board HQ 064
Fitzwilliam Street

F
5 Scarlet Row 082
5 Scarlet Row
Essex Street West
T 672 9534
eileenshields.com
Fallon & Byrne 048
11-17 Exchequer Street
T 472 1000
fallonandbyrne.com
Fine Design 084
Unit 34
The Design Tower
Grand Canal Quay
T 670 3699
finedesign.ie
Four Courts 010
Inns Quay
T 872 5555

G
Gallery of Photography 066
Meeting House Square
T 671 4654
galleryofphotography.ie
GPO 015
O'Connell Street
Grogan's 040
15 William Street South
T 677 9320
L'Gueuleton 062
1 Fade Street
T 675 3708
lgueuleton.com

H
Hogan's 058
35 South Great George's Street
T 677 5904
The Horseshoe Bar 050
The Shelbourne
27 St Stephen's Green North
T 663 4500
marriott.com
Hugh Lane Gallery 034
Charlemont House
Parnell Square North
T 222 5550
hughlane.ie

I
The International Bar 038
23 Wicklow Street
T 677 9250
international-bar.com

J

James Joyce Centre 032
35 North Great George's Street
T 878 8547
jamesjoyce.ie

James Ussher Library 074
Trinity College

Jenny Vander 080
50 Drury Street
T 677 0406

Joanne Hynes 080
T 087 993 2107
joannehynes.com

K

Kehoe's 052
9 Anne Street South
T 677 8312

Kilkenny 080
6 Nassau Street
T 677 7066
www.kilkennyshop.com

Kilmainham Gaol 032
Inchicore Road
T 453 5984

Krystle 060
21-25 Harcourt Street
T 478 4066
krystlenightclub.com

L

Lansdowne Road 090
Lansdowne Road
T 238 2300
www.lrsdc.ie

Lara Lu Foods 062
1 George's Street Arcade
T 087 990 8003
laralufoods.com

Leopardstown Racecourse 094
Leopardstown
T 289 0500
www.leopardstown.com

Lillies Bordello 060
Adam Court
Grafton Street
T 769 9204
lilliesbordello.com

Locks 046
1 Windsor Terrace
T 454 3391
locksrestaurant.ie

The Long Hall 040
51 South Great George's Street
T 475 1590

M

Mandala Spa 092
La Stampa Hotel
35 Dawson Street
T 677 4444
mandala.ie

The Mermaid Café 041
69-70 Dame Street
T 670 8236
mermaid.ie

Milk + Cookies 080
14 Westbury Mall
T 671 0104
milkandcookiesdublin.com

The Mound of Light 102
Oulart Hill
County Wexford

N
National Aquatic Centre 089
  Snugborough Road
  T 646 4300
  nationalaquaticcentre.ie
Nude 033
  21 Suffolk Street
  T 677 4804
  nude.ie

O
Odessa 054
  14 Dame Court
  T 670 7634
  odessa.ie
O'Driscoll Furniture 081
  26-28 Lombard Street East
  T 671 1069
  oddesign.com

P
Pia Bang Home 042
  2 Anne Street South
  T 888 3777
  piabang.ie

R
Restaurant Patrick Guilbaud 051
  21 Upper Merrion Street
  T 676 4192
  restaurantpatrickguilbaud.ie

S
Sheridans Cheesemongers 080
  11 Anne Street South
  T 679 3143
  sheridanscheesemongers.com
The Spire 013
  O'Connell Street/Henry Street

The Stag's Head 040
  1 Dame Court
  T 679 3687
  thestagshead.ie

T
Tea Room 053
  The Clarence
  6-8 Wellington Quay
  T 407 0813
  theclarence.ie
Thornton's 057
  Fitzwilliam Hotel
  128 St Stephen's Green
  T 478 7008
  fitzwilliamhotel.com
Trinity College 064
  College Green
  T 896 1000
  tcd.ie
Trocadero 038
  4 St Andrew Street
  T 677 5545
  trocadero.ie

U
Unicorn 042
  12b Merrion Court
  T 676 2182
  unicornrestaurant.com

W
The Winding Stair 045
  40 Ormond Quay
  T 872 7320
  www.winding-stair.com

HOTELS
ADDRESSES AND ROOM RATES

Bellinter House 097
Room rates:
double, from €180;
duplex, from €250;
double (main house), from €300
Navan
County Meath
T 046 903 0900
bellinterhouse.com

The Clarence 028
Room rates:
double, from €370;
Penthouse Suite, €2,700
6-8 Wellington Quay
T 407 0800
theclarence.ie

The Dylan 024
Room rates:
double, from €395
Eastmoreland Place
T 660 3000
dylan.ie

Europa 096
Room rates:
double, £200
Great Victoria Street
Belfast
T 00 44 28 9027 1066
www.hastingshotels.com

The Fitzwilliam 027
Room rates:
double, €370;
Superior Room, €400
St Stephen's Green
T 478 7000
fitzwilliamhotel.com

Glencomeragh House 098
Room rates:
double, €100
Clonmel
County Tipperary
T 052 33 181
glencomeragh.ie

Grafton House 030
Room rates:
double, from €115;
Room 14, from €120;
Penthouse Apartment, from €280
26-27 South Great George's Street
T 679 2041
graftonguesthouse.com

Malmaison 096
Room rates:
double, from €150
34-38 Victoria Street
Belfast
T 00 44 28 9022 0200
malmaison-belfast.com

Marlfield House 102
Room rates:
double, from €210
Courtown Road
Gorey
County Wexford
T 053 942 1124
marlfieldhouse.com

The Merrion 022
  Room rates:
  double, from €470;
  Junior Suite King, €950
  21 Merrion Street Upper
  T 603 0600
  merrionhotel.com
The Morgan 018
  Room rates:
  double, from €150;
  King Deluxe 228, from €195
  10 Fleet Street
  T 643 7000
  themorgan.com
The Morrison 020
  Room rates:
  double, from €165;
  Riverview Room, from €165;
  Penthouse Suite, €2,000
  Ormond Quay
  T 887 2400
  www.morrisonhotel.ie
Number 31 017
  Room rates:
  double, from €220;
  Superior Double, from €260
  31 Leeson Close
  T 676 5011
  number31.ie
Rathsallagh House 088
  Room rates:
  double, €135
  Dunlavin
  County Wicklow
  T 045 403 112
  rathsallaghhousehotel.com

The Shelbourne 026
  Room rates:
  double, from €220;
  Deluxe, from €230;
  Princess Grace Suite, €2,500
  27 St Stephen's Green
  T 663 4500
  marriott.com
La Stampa Hotel 046
  Room rates:
  double, from €140
  35 Dawson Street
  T 677 4444
  lastampa.ie

WALLPAPER* CITY GUIDES

Editorial Director
Richard Cook

Art Director
Loran Stosskopf
Editor
Rachael Moloney
Author
Paul McCann
Deputy Editor
Jeremy Case
Managing Editor
Jessica Diamond

Chief Designer
Daniel Shrimpton
Designer
Lara Collins
Map Illustrator
Russell Bell

Photography Editor
Sophie Corben
Photography Assistant
Robin Key

Sub-Editors
Chloë Chapman
Melanie Parr
Delicia Smith

Editorial Assistant
Ella Marshall

Interns
Daniel Lewis
Karen Smith

Wallpaper* Group
Editor-in-Chief
Tony Chambers
Publishing Director
Gord Ray
Publisher
Neil Sumner

Contributors
Sara Henrichs
Meirion Pritchard
Ellie Stathaki

Wallpaper* ® is a
registered trademark
of IPC Media Limited

All prices are correct at
time of going to press,
but are subject to change.

PHAIDON

Phaidon Press Limited
Regent's Wharf
All Saints Street
London N1 9PA

Phaidon Press Inc
180 Varick Street
New York, NY 10014

Phaidon® is a registered
trademark of Phaidon
Press Limited

www.phaidon.com

First published 2008
© 2008 IPC Media Limited

ISBN 978 0 7148 4896 9

A CIP Catalogue record for
this book is available from
the British Library.

Printed in China

PHOTOGRAPHERS

David Cordner/Alamy
GPO, p015

Erol Gemma
Four Courts, pp010-011
Dubin Castle, p012
Custom House, p014
Number 31, p017
The Morrison, p020, p021
The Merrion, pp022-023
The Shelbourne, p026
The Fitzwilliam, p027
The Clarence, pp028-029
Grafton House, pp030-031
Nude, p033
Eden, p036
The International
Bar, pp038-039
The Mermaid Café, p041
Bang Café, pp042-043
The Winding Stair, p045
Locks, p046
Bewley's Oriental
Café, p047
Fallon & Byrne, pp048-049
The Horseshoe Bar, p050
Restaurant Patrick
Guilbaud, p051
Kehoe's, p052
Tea Room, p053
Odessa, pp054-055
Anseo, p056
Thornton's, p057
Hogan's, p058
Doheny & Nesbitt, p059
Krystle, pp060-061

Maria MacVeigh, p063
Alto Vetro, p065
Meeting House Square,
pp066-067
Central Bank of Ireland,
pp070-071
Berkeley Library,
pp072-073
Department of Finance,
pp076-077
5 Scarlet Row, pp082-083
Croke Park Stadium,
pp090-091
Mandala Spa, pp092-093

Ros Kavanagh
Glencomeragh House,
pp098-099, pp100-101

Paul McCarthy
Busáras, pp068-069
Bank of Ireland HQ,
pp078-079

**Donal Murphy
Photography**
Chester Beatty
Library, p037
Leopardstown Racecourse,
pp094-095

Vincent O'Byrne/Alamy
Dublin city view, inside
front cover

Perry Ogdan
Hugh Lane Gallery,
pp034-035

DUBLIN
A COLOUR-CODED GUIDE TO THE HOT 'HOODS

THE LIBERTIES AND KILMAINHAM
This ungentrified slice of old Dublin is filled with antiques shops and traditional boozers

CENTRAL SOUTH
Away from the chain stores, join the glam crowd in chichi bistros and members' clubs

CENTRAL NORTH
Three unmissable landmarks reward the intrepid who venture north of the River Liffey

GEORGIAN DUBLIN
Nestled among the genteel terraces and swanky squares is the city's epicurean epicentre

TRINITY COLLEGE
A succession of far-sighted university grandees have left a legacy of radical architecture

DOCKLANDS
The once-desolate Grand Canal Dock is the focus of the regeneration of this portside area

RANELAGH AND BALLSBRIDGE
Dublin's affluent southern suburbs buzz with bars and restaurants for the newly monied

TEMPLE BAR
Sidestep the stags and hens to discover high-end boutiques and engaging art galleries

For a full description of each neighbourhood, see the Introduction.
Featured venues are colour-coded, according to the district in which they are located.